Sportsviewers Guide
MOTOR RACING

Alan Henry

DAVID & CHARLES
Newton Abbot   London

Contents

British Library Cataloguing in Publication Data
Henry, Alan
    Motor racing. — (Sportsviewers guides)
    1. Automobile racing
    I. Title   II. Series
    796.7′2   GV1029

    ISBN 0-7153-8535-6

The Sportsviewers' Guide to Motor racing was produced and designed by Siron Publishing Limited of 20 Queen Anne Street, London W1
Series editor: Nicholas Keith
Photographs by Tommy Hindley and Tony Henshaw of Professional Sport.
Designed by Ann Doolan

Typeset by ABM Typographics Ltd, Hull and printed by Printer Industria Gráfica SA Cuatro Caminos, Apartado 8, Sant Vincenç dels Horts, Barcelona, Spain DLB 36114-1983 for David & Charles (Publishers) Limited Brunel House   Newton Abbot   Devon

Foreword

When I'm doing a commentary on a motor race I often wonder how many of my audience fully understand what I'm talking about! Very few I suspect. Although motor racing is an action-packed and thrilling sport with enormous visual appeal it is also very complicated and really needs a thorough knowledge and understanding of its regulations, history, personalities and politics for viewers to get the most out of it.

I therefore welcome this book which simply, but concisely and comprehensively, provides a most entertaining explanation of what motor racing is about. It has been my pleasure to know the author, Alan Henry, for a long time during which I've not only valued his friendship but learned a lot from his authoritative, penetrating — and provocative — books on motor racing and his regular contributions to two of Britain's leading publications, *Motor Sport* and *Motoring News*.

As well as the history and development of motor racing, its rules, technology, venues and personalities,

Alan outlines how to get to the top if you've got what it takes — and how much you might earn if you get there — a fascinating revelation!

I enjoyed reading his *Sportsviewers Guide to Motor Racing* immensely and look forward to answering a greatly reduced number of questioning letters following the success I'm sure it will achieve.

Murray Walker

3

History and development

From the moment the first fledgling 'horseless carriages' spluttered into life around the turn of the century, there have always been some ambitious, enterprising and enthusiastic individuals whose overwhelming ambition was to drive faster — and for longer — than any of their rivals. It is, therefore, not surprising that these motoring pioneers involved themselves in record-breaking runs and other forms of competition long before the automobile became an everyday part of the man-in-the-street's way of life.

Novelty, a spirit of adventure and a certain element of chaos characterised the early days of motor racing. Most of these pioneering events took place on unsurfaced open roads choked with stones and dust. Early events which attracted a great deal of interest included such epics as the Paris–Madrid race. However, such niceties as crowd control and discipline were unheard of and, when a number of onlookers were killed by out-of-control machines in the 1906 Paris–Bordeaux race, it began to become apparent that smaller, organised circuit races would shape the sport's pattern in the years that followed.

The first 'Grand Prix' was held near Le Mans in 1906, participants being required to run 12 laps of a 103 km track over a period of 2 days. It was this and similar events, held under the auspices of the Automobile Club de France, which helped lay the foundations of the French pre-eminence in matters motoring — and led to motor sport's governing body establishing its home in that country.

Over the years that followed, the complexion of international motor racing changed markedly with the

Monsieur Gabriel sets a record in winning the 1903 Paris–Madrid race in 5hrs 18mins (BBC Hulton Picture Library).

Malcolm Campbell in his Sunbeam at Pendine Sands in 1924 (BBC Hulton Picture Library)

times. The era of the well-heeled, amateur sportsmen of the 1920s gave way to the nationalistic flag-waving of the following decade when government finance from Hitler's Germany helped Mercedes-Benz and Auto Union to the very pinnacle of international Grand Prix success. Britain's participation at this time was confined to well-intentioned, but poorly financed organisations such as ERA. They were not short on racing knowledge, but could hardly be expected to match the German budgets from their slender private resources and were relegated to the role of also-rans as a consequence.

Technical progress on the part of the new motor manufacturers provided a persuasive justification behind early motor racing involvements — and names such as Renault, Fiat and Mercedes were as familiar in the motor racing firmament before the First World War as they were to be after the Second. After the First World War, limits in engine capacity and in weight went some way towards codifying technical regulations. These were to be refined over the following two decades, with single-seater, out-and-out Grand Prix racing cars gradually asserting their individual identity.

In the 1920s it had been commonplace for production-based sports cars to double up as Grand Prix cars in the interests of economy, but sports cars were going their own way by the 1930s and events such as the Le Mans 24 hour race were to become as important as any Grand Prix in the years that followed. It should also be noted that, before the Second World War, motor racing was of a largely national character and its international flavour was nowhere near as pronounced as it has become in the years since 1945.

Between 1907 and 1939, with the exception of a handful of international Grands Prix run on the Donington Park road circuit, the centre of British motor racing was Brooklands, the oval 'speed bowl' built near Weybridge by a wealthy businessman. European racing was a rather more gregarious affair, because of geographical convenience.

Motor racing quickly grew into one of the century's most compelling spectator sports. Those who consider that it has only been 'big business' since the advent of commercial sponsorship in the 1970s and '80s would be amazed to learn of the amount of national media attention which surrounded, say, the visits of the Auto Union and Mercedes-Benz teams to the 1938 and 1939 Donington Grands Prix. Inevitably, the crowds had their favourites and British fans of that time followed the achievements of their heroes — such as the dashing record-breaker Sir Malcolm Campbell and the youthful Dick Seaman — with the sort of enthusiasm which tennis and golf stars attract today.

The technology behind the all-conquering German machines was something at which their rivals marvelled, but teutonic efficiency was to be applied to a very different purpose before very long: not only motor racing would change beyond all recognition by the end of the following decade.

International motor racing received an enormous boost in 1950 when a formal World Championship was instigated. This enabled the achievements of the sport's participants to be gauged against each other and some spectacular, talented personalities burst onto the post-war scene, not all of whom needed the World Championship points table to indicate their sheer class. In the 1950s, the quiet Argentine driver, Juan-Manuel Fangio, won five World Championships in brilliant style before retiring at the age of 46 mid-way through 1958. His record tally of twenty-four

Grand Prix victories stood for another decade before being beaten by the shy, retiring Scottish border farmer who is still regarded by many as the greatest driver of all time — Jim Clark. His record of twenty-five wins was later exceeded by his compatriot, Jackie Stewart — and the record now stands to him with twenty-seven victories.

Yet, race victories and championships apart, it would be a brave man who said that any of these drivers was *better* than Britain's Stirling Moss. Relishing the role of the underdog, this brilliant son of a London dentist chose to drive British cars in the early 1950s when competitive machinery was only available from European constructors. If Moss had come onto the scene ten years later the story might have been very different. As it was, a crash at Goodwood in 1962 cut short his career at the age of 33 and the motor sporting fraternity was denied the spectacle of seeing Moss and Clark facing each other from the cockpit of equal cars.

In a sport as complex as this — in which the participants' success depends so crucially on the equipment they are using — it is hardly surprising that the most successful car constructors quickly became surrounded by an aura and mystique matching those of the drivers themselves. Although the Alfa Romeo marque dominated the immediate post-war years, providing Farina and Fangio with their championship-winning mounts in 1950 and 1951, it was a rival Italian team which was to establish a reputation as perhaps the most famous racing organisation of all — Ferrari. Founded by Enzo Ferrari, the pre-war Alfa Romeo racing manager, the team has now been competing successfully — and winning — for almost thirty years.

Nelson Piquet, the 1983 world champion, celebrates his victory in the European GP.

9

The teams of Mercedes-Benz (who made a fleeting return to the Formula 1 stage in 1954 and 1955), Maserati and Ferrari dominated the 1950s until Britain came to establish herself as a force to be reckoned with. Britain's immediate post-war effort had been the BRM organisation, but the bureaucratic, committee-operated team so frustrated one of its members that he broke away to establish his own team to carry Britain's colours to Grand Prix victory. He was Tony Vandervell, an industrial magnate and bearing king, whose green Vanwalls finally won the World Championship for Constructors in 1958 — although the drivers' title fell to Britain's Mike Hawthorn, driving a Ferrari.

The efforts of Vanwall and BRM

John Cooper revolutionised the single-seater racing car when he put the engine behind the driver — and there it has stayed to this day. Next, it was the era of Colin Chapman and his Lotuses, blazing a trail of technical genius, the culmination of which was the development of 'ground effect' designs in the mid-1970s. This harnessing of the airflow beneath the car literally stuck them to the road and the principle eventually resulted in such madly spiralling lap speeds that the sport's governing body, FISA (Fédération Internationale Sport Automobile) eventually had to step in and effectively ban 'ground effect'.

Motor racing's post-war popularity has not been confined to the Grand Prix arena. Other categories, such as endurance racing (sports cars), saloon car championships and the lesser single-seater racing car categories — Formula 2, 3 and Ford etc. — have prospered hand-in-hand with the general increase of commercial interest in the sport. The United States, however, while supporting rounds of most international championships, also retains enormously popular domestic categories such as NASCAR saloon racing and CART Indy car racing, neither of which has ever made an impact beyond her shores.

The advent of commercial sponsorship on the cars in the 1970s largely took the control of international motor racing's finances out of the hands of its traditional paymasters, the fuel and tyre companies. But the onrush of money into the sport certainly helped to increase its popularity, even though the purists saw it as something of a double-edged sword. Traditional sporting values may have been jeopardised in the motor racing arena — but there is no doubt that racing is bigger, brighter and technically more interesting as a result.

Stirling Moss at Silverstone in 1956 (BBC Hulton Picture Library).

(who were to establish themselves, briefly, as a competitive force between 1962 and 1965) laid the foundation for a largely British domination of the international scene which lasted for much of the 1960s and 1970s. Britain's

Rules

The rules governing international motor racing are codified and controlled by the Paris-based Fédération Internationale de l'Automobile, an organisation representing automobile clubs all over the world. The FIA does not confine itself to governing automobile sport, but holds sway on all manner of activities connected with motoring and the motor car on a worldwide basis. The FIA has a number of working groups which specialise in such areas as touring, road traffic problems, customs matters and technical and environmental considerations in addition to motor sporting questions which concern us here. It is the International Motor Sport Federation (FISA) which is the working group responsible to the FIA in this particular respect.

Each year the FIA publishes a comprehensive set of international regulations by which the conduct of every national and international sporting event is guided. Apart from such things as technical regulations — which lay down the specifications within which cars for certain categories must be built (e.g. Formula 1 and Group C sports racing cars)— there are also exhaustive rules. These cover the conduct of the race meeting on the day and the facilities which must be provided at the circuit on which the meeting is being held.

At the top international level, these standards are extremely high and are inspected regularly by a full-time official of the FISA who spends all his time travelling the world and submitting long, detailed reports to the governing body after inspections. On a circuit staging a World Championship Grand Prix, for example, there is a mass of painstakingly precise details which have to be covered.

The track surface must be a prescribed width; guard rails have to be erected to a precise and unvarying

Rene Arnoux visits the pits . . . and the protective headgear worn by modern drivers.

specification; and run-off areas on fast corners must incorporate catch-fencing in order to restrain a wayward car, as the safety of the paying spectator is deemed, rightly, to be of paramount importance. The circuit must be staffed by an appropriate number of marshals, almost always unpaid but highly skilled amateurs, and fire-fighting equipment is subject to regular stringent checks.

Such has been the concern over

steadily increasing Formula 1 lap speeds over the past few years, that major international tracks are now only licensed for three years at a time, after which they must be subject to another major inspection — and perhaps be obliged to spend hundreds of thousands of pounds updating their facilities in line with the latest thinking on safety trends.

13

Rules/2

The section on technology underlines just what high technical standards are required from the racing car builders, but the rules covering driver disciplines are equally onerous. In a sport as potentially hazardous as motor racing they must be, although it should be emphasised that few drivers have reached the top without demonstrating a degree of consideration for their rivals; the occasional maverick still gets away with unruly behaviour in the sport's upper echelons but,

generally, the rules enable such behaviour to be stamped on by the authorities at an early stage.

To the untrained observer, the rough and tumble of an international motor race may well seem like unbridled chaos. But the FIA's Code of Driving Conduct is specific about how competitors should behave, and contravention of this code can bring sharp retribution. While a driver may use the full width of the circuit when he is driving alone, the moment he is

In a tight corner: F1 cars jostle for position at Brands Hatch.

to control competitors' behaviour: a waved blue flag, for example, will indicate to a competitor that he should give way to a much faster car which is coming up behind. A waved yellow flag will indicate danger, possibly an accident ahead, and a black flag, shown with the car's individual race number, means that the driver should stop at the pits at the end of the next lap. The penalty for disregarding any of these flags can be disqualification, a fine or even suspension.

There is a system of justice within motor sport, and a competitor who feels aggrieved by the decision of any such tribunal can appeal against a penalty imposed. His appeal first goes to the national club (the RAC in Britain, for example) and then to the FISA's court of appeal in Paris. The sport's statutes theoretically preclude any dissatisfied competitor from pursuing a further remedy in the civil courts, but such is the money involved today in Grand Prix racing that some teams and drivers have done just that — usually without success.

The regulations covering the various categories for racing cars are written with painstaking thoroughness, but there will always be ambiguities of interpretation when a car's competitiveness may depend on being constructed as closely to the outer limits of the rules as possible. A year or so ago, Grand Prix racing was rocked to its core by a major dispute between British teams and the FISA when one innovative designer read the rule books very carefully and devised a method of running his car below the minimum weight limit during the course of the race itself.

The rules at that time allowed the car to be presented for a post-race weight check with all its regular fluid contents, apart from petrol, (i.e. oil and water) at their 'normal' levels. Thus it had become the practice to top

caught up by another car which is 'temporarily or constantly faster', he must give the other vehicle the right of way. Deliberate baulking of other competitors is also prohibited, although this can be very difficult to prove in the close competition of Formula 1.

There is a comprehensive system of flag signals employed by race officials

Rules/3

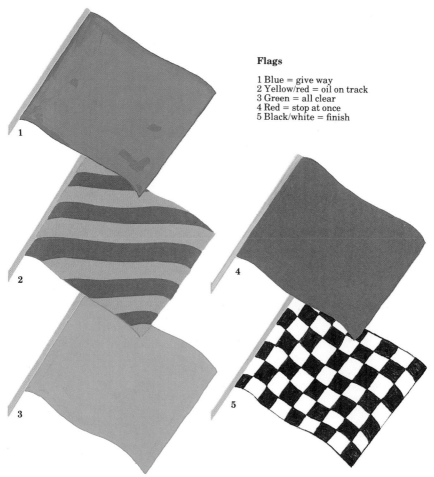

Flags

1 Blue = give way
2 Yellow/red = oil on track
3 Green = all clear
4 Red = stop at once
5 Black/white = finish

up water and oil tanks to ensure that the car would comfortably pass the weight check. This designer realised that it would be (apparently) legal to run water tanks for 'brake cooling purposes': the water would, in effect, be used up on the opening lap, leaving the now substantially lightened car to run its entire race distance in a far more competitive trim than before. After the race, the water level in the tank would be topped up again, the car presented for its weight check and emerge with an official seal of approval.

The decision of the Brabham and Williams team to employ such tactics resulted in their cars being disqualified from first and second places in the 1982 Brazilian Grand Prix. Moreover, the resultant indignation which stemmed from the FISA court of appeal's refusal to reverse the disqualification decision nearly split Formula 1 straight down the middle. Fortunately, this was a particularly dramatic example of disputes which can erupt over the rules within motor racing, most such arguments arising from lesser grumbles and complaints.

Glossary

CART
Championship Auto Racing Teams, association of American teams involved in 'Indy car' racing in the US, mainly specialised and highly spectacular events held on oval 'speed bowls'.

ERA
English Racing Automobile.

FIA
Fédération Internationale de l'Automobile, ultimate governing body of international motorsport.

FISA
The International Motor Sports Federation (Fédération Internationale Sport Automobile), to whom the FIA delegates the responsibility of administering motorsport.

FOCA
The Formula One Constructors' Association, a commercial association of predominantly British-based Grand Prix teams concerned with offering a complete competing 'package' to race organisers. Also responsible for negotiating prize funds for grand prix events.

Homologation
Acceptance of a specified production car to an international racing category which demands that proof of construction of a certain specified number of cars be furnished by the manufacturer. e.g. in saloon car Group A racing, Rover had to produce 5,000 examples of its 3500 saloon within a 12-month period in order for the car to be homologated.

NASCAR
National Stock Car Racing Association, not to be confused with 'stock cars' in the accepted English sense. This is the governing body of the big saloon car racing championship which is tremendously popular in South Eastern US. The high spot of its season is the Daytona 500 race, held on the banked Florida speedway of that name, which reputedly attracts television audiences second only to the Super Bowl football matches throughout North America.

RAC
Royal Automobile Club, national organisation governing motor sport within Great Britain.

Scrutineering
Pre- and post-race inspection mandatory for all competing cars to ensure that they conform with technical and safety regulations applicable to their category.

Mario Andretti (US)
Born: 28 February 1940
World champion: 1978
Mario Andretti's life story has about it
the essence of the great American
dream. Born in Trieste in the early
months of the Second World War,
Mario's family spent the first seven
years of his life in a displaced persons'
camp before emigrating to the United
States in 1955. His passion for racing
was fuelled by childhood memories of
the Mille Miglia road race in his
native land and he carried that
enthusiasm across the Atlantic —
where he scratched and clawed his
way into the professional motor racing
game.

He won his first Indianapolis 500 in
1969, his first Grand Prix (for Ferrari)
in 1971 and the World Championship
(for Lotus) in 1978. One of the most
versatile men ever to sit in a racing
car, as well as one of the most civil and

Mario Andretti (left): versatile.

Jean-Marie Balestre: demonstrative.

courteous, Andretti realised another
milestone in his tireless ambition
when he shared a Porsche 956 in the
1983 Le Mans 24-hour sports car race
with his 20-year old son, Michael.
They finished a magnificent third!

Jean-Marie Balestre (France)
Ambitious and politically inclined,
Balestre is the French president of the
sport's governing body, the Fédération
Internationale Sport Automobile
(FISA). A successful businessman,
Balestre's stand in recent years has
been designed to keep the sport's
administration within FISA's domain
— and to prevent the Ecclestone-
organised constructors' association
(FOCA) expanding its interest beyond
purely commercial horizons. He has
clashed with Ecclestone on several
well-publicised occasions, but has suc-
ceeded in keeping a balance between
the FISA and FOCA forces. Dramatic,
demonstrative and extrovert, Balestre
is one of many strong personalities on
the motor racing landscape today.

Derek Bell (GB)
Born: 31 October 1941
Winner: Le Mans, 1975, 1981 and 1982
The perpetually youthful looks of Derek Bell have been a popular feature on the international racing scene ever since 1968 when he set out on his full-time professional career in an F2 Brabham. Despite a stint with Ferrari in 1969, Bell's single-seater career never quite gelled, but this good-looking Englishman consolidated his position as a top-class sports car driver with three wins at Le Mans and was still a member of the prestigious works Porsche team in 1983.

Derek Bell: popular features.

Colin Chapman (GB)

Energetic, dynamic and endowed with immense drive, Colin Chapman was one of the few really original thinkers in the ranks of post-war racing car designers. Afer leaving the RAF in 1947, Chapman built his first Austin Seven-based special with the aid of a £25 loan from his girlfriend, Hazel, later his wife. In the early 1950s he founded the Lotus company — building light, agile sports cars — and entered Grand Prix competition in 1958.

He pioneered the monocoque chassis construction (1962), became the first team owner to use the powerful Ford-financed Cosworth V8 engine (1967) and totally rewrote the parameters of racing car performance with the harnessing of under-car air flow to produce 'ground effect' (1977). His cars won countless Grands Prix over the past two decades and there is scarcely an area of motor racing design which has not been touched by Chapman's influence. He also built up the Lotus road car company into a highly regarded organisation before

Colin Chapman: original thinker.

his sudden death, in December 1982, which deprived the sport of a remarkable personality.

Jim Clark (GB)
Born: 14 March 1936
World champion: 1963 and 1965

When Jim Clark died in a minor Formula 2 race at Hockenheim in the spring of 1968, the whole fabric of international motor racing trembled. Clark, more than anybody else in the history of motor racing, had seemed totally inviolate. His partnership with the mercurial Lotus boss, Colin Chapman, epitomised F1 success for much of the 1960s, for they thought alike and each displayed a consummate natural brilliance in their individual fields.

Jim Clark was a shy, self-effacing son of a Scottish border farmer and he went motor racing primarily for pleasure. He was the last great sporting 'amateur' driver and died just before the onset of unbridled commercialism (which he abhorred) in the sport he loved so passionately. The record books show he won the World Championship title in 1963 and 1965, but he came within a whisker of taking it in 1962 and 1964 as well. The fact of the matter is that he dominated all four seasons in a manner seldom matched since.

The green Lotus with its yellow stripe and blue-helmeted driver won a total of twenty-five Grands Prix between the start of 1962 and his death in 1968. But it was the manner of Clark's success which demoralised his opposition. Inevitably starting from pole position, he would destroy his competitors' spirit with a searing first lap that none of them could approach, let alone equal. He was a yardstick by which others judged their own performance and he had most of them psychologically beaten before they even climbed into their cars.

21

The Stars/3

Bernie Ecclestone (GB)
A self-made millionaire who amassed fortunes through motor trading and a multitude of property deals, Ecclestone is a compact, dapper South London businessman who used to race motorcycles and Formula 3 cars in the immediate post-war years. In the late 1960s he applied his business management knowledge to the world of motor racing and, after buying the Brabham Formula 1 team at the end of 1971, quickly became the most powerful and commercially influential man in the Grand Prix game. A leading light in the Formula One Constructors' Association (FOCA), Ecclestone's tireless business mind has negotiated Grand Prix prize funds and television coverage contracts for much of the past decade. Autocratic, a workaholic and a mental mathematician of considerable guile, Ecclestone is not everybody's friend — but his contribution to motor racing's prosperity is beyond doubt.

Juan-Manuel Fangio (Argentina)
Born: 24 June 1911
World champion: 1951, 1954–7
There is a strong case for arguing that this mild-mannered, modest Argentine was the greatest racing driver of all time. Juan-Manuel Fangio came to Europe in 1948 after making a name in his homeland driving rugged Ford-based specials in bumpy, dusty prewar road races. His delicate touch, magical judgement and unwavering consistency set him apart from his contemporaries from the outset of his Grand Prix career.

Over 40 when he won his first World Championship for Alfa Romeo in 1951, Fangio went on to win four more titles for Mercedes-Benz (1954–5), Ferrari (1956) and Maserati (1957). He was a sensitive tactician and a great gentleman: when his youthful teammate, Stirling Moss, won the

Bernie Ecclestone (above): powerful.

Juan-Manuel Fangio (right): magical judgement (BBC Hulton Picture Library).

1955 British Grand Prix at Aintree, Fangio's sister Mercedes was only a few feet behind in second place. To this day, Moss has never been quite sure whether he beat Fangio fair and square or whether the great champion allowed him to take a significant triumph on home soil.

But Fangio was no soft touch. Two

years later, at the age of 46, his Maserati defeated the English Ferrari team drivers, Mike Hawthorn and Peter Collins (both some twenty years his junior), in a sensational climb back through the field in the German Grand Prix. Fangio smashed the daunting Nurburgring's lap record six times in the process.

Fangio started the 1958 season driving a reduced programme of selected races for Maserati, but, after the French Grand Prix, came to the conclusion that it was time to retire. He returned to his native Argentina, where he had substantial business interests, but remains a distinguished member of the international racing fraternity and still makes occasional forays to European races.

Enzo Ferrari (Italy)

Individualistic, unpredictable and autocratic, Enzo Ferrari rules the automotive dynasty which has carried his name since the early 1940s. A racing driver himself in the 1920s, Ferrari progressed to the point where

Jacky Ickx: civilised.

he was running the Alfa Romeo factory racing effort under his own team's banner, splitting with the established Italian marque after a disagreement over the cars' performance just before the war.

He then established his own car company in his home town of Modena and, by 1948, the first Formula 1 Ferraris were ready to take to the circuits. In 1951, Froilan Gonzales drove the first Ferrari team to victory in the British Grand Prix, ironically vanquishing the Alfas. From that moment onwards the team has not looked back. The list of those who have driven Ferraris over the ensuing three decades reads like a 'who's who' of motor racing, and world championships fell to the team in 1952, 1953, 1956, 1961, 1964, 1975, 1976, 1977, 1979, 1982 and 1983.

It has always been acknowledged that the engines were the most remarkable aspects of Ferrari's cars, generally running with a precision and reliability that has been the envy of his rivals, even though the chassis have not always been the best. Fiat took over the controlling financial stake in Ferrari's empire during 1969, but 'the old man' still presides over the racing business to this day. Born in 1898, he is a withdrawn, dignified and very private man, still haunted with grief over the death of his only son, Dino, in 1955.

Jacky Ickx (Belgium)
Born: 1 January 1945
Winner: Le Mans, 1969, 1975–7, 1981–2
Civilised, articulate and talented, Jacky Ickx's early motor racing exploits marked him down as a potential future champion long before he ever sat in a Grand Prix car. But, somehow, World Championship laurels never fell in this pleasant Belgian driver's direction, despite some brilliant drives as Ferrari's team leader of 1970–2. But Ickx has become a legend in the specialist world of long distance sports car racing, winning Le Mans six times — a record unmatched by anybody.

Alan Jones (Australia)
Born: 2 November 1946
World champion: 1980
The son of Stan Jones, a famous postwar Australian racing star, Alan was fired with a passion for motor racing from an early age. When his father raced Maseratis and Coopers 'down under' in the 1950s, the short-trousered Jones Jnr would always be there to watch and, to a great extent, this hard-bitten youngster was spurred on in his ambition to become world champion by his father's success in Australasia.

It was a long, hard slog for Jones to

Enzo Ferrari (LAT Photographic)

Alan Jones: determined.

get into a position where a decent F1 drive became a realistic proposition for him. He came to Britain in the early 1970s and struggled through the junior formulae before getting his Grand Prix break at the wheel of a private Hesketh in 1975. Even at this stage he did not look a 'natural', but he was obviously endowed with enormous strength and determination. When a lucky break provided him with a chance of a drive in the Shadow team, he underlined his ability by scoring his first victory in the 1977 Austrian Grand Prix.

In 1978 he signed up with Frank Williams and the two grew in stature together, Jones taking the World Championship at the wheel of the superb, ground-effect Williams FW07 in 1980. He stayed on with Williams the following year and, although unlucky not to retain his title, rounded off his career with a fine victory at Las Vegas.

He then retired, ostensibly to look after his farm and other business interests in Australia. But he kept his hand in, driving Porsche sports cars in the 1982 Australian national championship, and eventually concluded that the lure of motor racing at international level was too much to resist. In the 1983 Long Beach Grand Prix, after a year's absence from the F1 stage, he made his return at the wheel of an Arrows A6. Despite the fact that one of his legs was pinned following a fracture sustained in a horse-riding accident only six weeks earlier, the blunt, uncompromising, fun-loving Australian proved that he had still got what it takes.

Niki Lauda (Austria)
Born: 22 February 1949
World champion: 1975 and 1977
One of motor racing's living legends, this slightly built Austrian mortgaged a life assurance policy to his bank in

Niki Lauda: living legend.

order to finance his first stab at Formula 1. It was the best investment he ever made. After building his reputation with the March and BRM teams, he joined Ferrari in 1974 and achieved spectacular success. After winning the 1975 championship he was badly burned during a high-speed crash in the 1976 German Grand Prix, but fought back from the edge of death to race again before the end of that season.

In 1977 Lauda regained the World Championship before splitting with Ferrari and in 1978 moving to Brabham where he never gained the same level of sustained success again. At the end of 1979, he abruptly retired from racing mid-way through practice for the Canadian Grand Prix, saying that his spark of enthusiasm had vanished. Although he concentrated on his fledgling airline business for the next two years, the attraction of motor racing was too much for Lauda: in 1982 he was back, and winning again, with the McLaren team.

In his heyday, Lauda applied a neatness of style and conscientious approach to his driving which seemed almost clinically ruthless. Supremely calm and even-tempered, he developed a sharp sense of humour early in his career which he still exhibits to his closest friends. A man full of contradictions and surprises.

Stirling Moss (GB)
Born: 17 September 1929
In the post-war motor racing world, Stirling Moss's patriotic approach to the sport mirrored the sort of nationalistic commitment exemplified by Battle of Britain fighter aces: taking on theoretically superior rivals, against the odds, and emerging triumphant. Unfortunately, it was Moss's fierce loyalty to British teams at a time when they were unable to provide him with a winning car which prevented him from winning the World Championship as his brilliance so richly deserved.

First, with a private Maserati

Stirling Moss (LAT Photographic)

bought by his father, a wealthy dentist, and, later, as a member of the Mercedes works team, Moss's talent and flair shone like a beacon of hope to British enthusiasts. But it was not until he teamed up with the millionaire industrialist, Tony Vandervell, to lead the Vanwall team in 1957, that he finally found a British car capable of doing his ability justice. In 1958 he was beaten by the Ferrari driver, Mike Hawthorn, in his quest for the championship and, after Vanwall's withdrawal, took the conscious decision to race less-than-competitive cars for private teams — notably those owned by Rob Walker.

At the Easter Monday 1962 Goodwood meeting, at the wheel of a private Lotus 24, his Grand Prix career came to an end as the result of a dreadful, inexplicable crash. A year later, after what must now be regarded as a very premature test drive, Moss took the decision to retire. If he had deferred the decision a little longer, it is likely that Stirling Moss would have continued racing through the 1960s — possibly for Ferrari, with whom he would surely have grasped the championship crown.

Nelson Piquet (Brazil)
Born: 17 August 1952
World champion: 1981 and 1983
This talented Brazilian was born Nelson Sauto-Maior but switched to using his mother's maiden name, Piquet, at an early stage in his career when he wanted to keep the fact he was motor racing from his parents. If his father had been allowed to have his way, Nelson would have been coached for a life in professional tennis, but the attraction of motor racing was too much. Making his way up from a grounding in kart racing, Nelson was dominating the British national

Nelson Piquet: intuitive.

Formula 3 scene by 1978 and made some intermittent F1 appearances with a couple of minor teams at the end of the same year.

However, his long-term promise was quickly recognised by the shrewd Brabham team owner, Bernie Ecclestone. Nelson signed for the team at the start of 1979 and has driven for them ever since, pipping the Williams driver, Carlos Reutemann, for the World Championship in the final race of the 1981 season. In 1983 he did the same thing to Alain Prost by clinching his second title at the last race at Kyalami.

A gifted, intuitive driver and blessed with a neat style, Nelson Piquet is now an even better driver than he was when he won the title in 1981 and few people were surprised that he repeated that success. Off the circuit, he tends to be a very private person — scrupulously polite and mixing a wry, European sense of humour with occasional flashes of volatile Latin temperament.

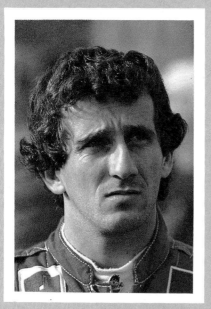

Alain Prost (left) and at the wheel of his Renault.

Alain Prost (France)
Born: 24 February 1955
A typical product of the recent French motor racing renaissance — largely sponsored by its national petrol company — Alain Prost has led the Renault team since the start of 1981.

A slight, quiet young man, Prost's appearance belies his speed and supremely smooth style behind the wheel.

In 1979 he served notice of his promise by winning the Monaco Grand Prix Formula 3 supporting race and was recruited into F1 with McLaren the following year. He admits that he has modelled his driving style on that of Jim Clark, but only when he joined Renault did he begin to demonstrate undeniable world-class form. One of the new breed of motor racing technocrats, he is uninspiring to see on the circuit, but most impressive against the stop watch. In 1983 he was pipped for the drivers' title in the last race by Piquet, having led for much of the season.

Keke Rosberg (Finland)
Born: 6 December 1948
World champion: 1982
When Alan Jones took the decision to retire abruptly at the end of the 1981 season, the Williams Grand Prix team was faced with a major problem over the task of recruiting a successor to the brilliant Australian. Eventually Williams signed up Rosberg, the Swedish-born Finn who had established a spectacular reputation in the lower echelons of the sport, but had been hampered by lack of a competitive car while serving out a two-year stint in the under-financed Fittipaldi F1 team.

Rosberg's early experience had been

gained in Formula Vee single-seaters and he gradually worked his way up the international motor racing ladder, scoring a significant victory in streaming wet conditions in the 1978 Silverstone International Trophy meeting. The Finn's lightning reflexes and tremendous wet-weather skill were highlighted in this race at the wheel of the Theodore F1 car. Even though Rosberg had achieved this success in his second F1 race, he vanquished only a modest level of opposition and his triumph could be regarded mainly as an interesting pointer to future form.

Keke Rosberg: impeccable taste.

Happily for the Williams team, Rosberg had lost none of that instant flair by the time he started the 1982 season, armed with a highly competitive car. At one point it seemed as though he might become the first world champion to take the title 'on points', without scoring a single Grand Prix victory, but he squeezed in a good win at the Swiss Grand Prix and clinched the title after beating off a challenge from Ulsterman John Watson in the final race of the year at Las Vegas.

Fastidious and endowed with expensive, but impeccable taste, Rosberg divides his free time between homes in Britain and Ibiza. Unlike so many of his predecessors, the taste of championship triumph in no way blunted Keke's thirst for success, and 1983 saw motor racing's top man driving with even more determination than ever to finish fifth in the drivers' championship.

Jackie Stewart (GB)
Born: 11 June 1939
World champion: 1969, 1971 and 1973
If anybody was responsible for transforming the image of motor racing from a specialised amateur stance to a level which matches professional golf, tennis and football, then it was this shrewd son of a Dumbarton garage owner. Jackie Stewart proved himself a gifted sportsman from an early age and came close to earning a position in the British Olympic clay pigeon shooting team long before he established his prowess behind the wheel of a racing car.

After dominating the British Formula 3 scene in 1964, Stewart graduated to Grand Prix racing the following year as a member of the BRM team alongside Graham Hill. It did not take long for him to gain a reputation as the most promising newcomer in the business. Although he won the 1965 Italian and 1966 Monaco Grands Prix for BRM, it was not until he joined Ken Tyrrell's fledgling F1 outfit at the start of 1968 that his career took off.

Driving first French Matras and later purpose-built Tyrrell machines exclusively for the British team owner, Stewart quickly donned the mantle of the late Jim Clark. Taking the world title in 1969, 1971 and 1973, he established an all-time record of twenty-seven Grand Prix victories which stands in the history books a decade later. Stewart finally hung up his helmet at the end of the 1973 season.

He debunked the myth that racing drivers should be devil-may-care extroverts to whom the risk of death or injury was a necessary part of their calling. His success brought with it influence in high places, so he quickly developed the weight to initiate sweeping improvements in safety standards, both from a circuit-facility and driver-equipment point of view. This attitude did not always find favour with the purists, and Jackie Stewart was much maligned as a result. But as European motor racing's first dollar millionaire, Stewart continues to this day as one of the sport's most informed observers, influential advisors and highly regarded PR figures.

Patrick Tambay (France)
Born: 25 June 1949
One of the most popular, courteous drivers in the business, Patrick Tambay's ability as an all-round sportsman is underlined by the fact

Jackie Stewart (LAT Photographic)

that he earned a place in the French national downhill skiing team while he was still at school. The son of a Paris building contractor, Patrick completed his education at the University of Colorado — which explains

Patrick Tambay: courteous.

the slight American 'twang' in his voice — before starting out on a motor racing career at the relatively late age of 23.

Tambay's progression to F1 was achieved by means of the series of Elf-financed Formula 2 teams which proliferated during the mid-1970s, making the route towards the top for French drivers significantly easier than their contemporaries. He made his Grand Prix debut at the wheel of a Theodore Ensign in 1977 before moving over to McLaren as James Hunt's teammate in 1978: unfortunately he did not prosper in the extrovert, aggressive McLaren environment and was dropped by the team at the end of 1979.

In 1980 he achieved a morale-

boosting triumph in the Can-Am sports car series in North America and eventually returned to F1 as a replacement for the late lamented Gilles Villeneuve at Ferrari in the middle of 1982. He cemented his relationship with the Italian team by winning that season's German Grand Prix and finally blossomed as a thinking, tactical, top-line contender with the powerful turbo cars from Maranello during 1983. A precise, accurate driver with a fluid style at the wheel he is never to be ignored as a potential winner and finished fourth in the 1983 championship.

Derek Warwick (GB)
Born: 27 August 1954
Widely regarded as one of Britain's brightest hopes for future World Championship honours, Warwick is one of the few professional drivers who has a full-time job when he is not strapped into the cockpit of his F1 car. As a director of his family's trailer-manufacturing business in Hampshire, Derek has a full business week between World Championship rounds. He started racing in stock cars, but graduated to F1 via Formula Ford, Formula 3 and Formula 2. His Grand Prix début for Toleman was in 1981 and he has remained loyal to this fledgling Formula 1 team which gave him his big F2 break in 1980. In the right car, Warwick is the man most likely to bring the drivers' championship title back to Britain.

John Watson (GB)
Born: 4 May 1946
Madly enthusiastic about motor racing from an early age, John Watson's rise from the Irish club racing scene to international Grand Prix stardom has been a long road. Born in Belfast, the son of a motor trader and amateur racer, he first got into F1 with a private Brabham in 1973. He won his

first Grand Prix in a Penske in 1976, but had to wait another five years before winning the British Grand Prix (his second triumph) at the wheel of a McLaren.

Unpredictable in the sense that his

Derek Warwick (top): British hope.

John Watson: British stalwart.

form can vary alarmingly, Watson is a perfectionist in the complicated business of 'setting up' his cars' chassis adjustments. If he is unhappy about his machine, then he can be less than inspired. If he hits top form, he can show championship quality. Beneath everything, however, Watson remains a total motor racing enthusiast.

Frank Williams (GB)

Frank Williams' entrepreneurial talent, allied to a passionate, all-pervading enthusiasm for motor racing, has established him as Britain's leading Grand Prix team owner of recent years. It has taken Williams, the son of a war-time bomber pilot, twenty years to progress from a penniless saloon car racer to a World Championship car constructor.

His qualities of initiative and hard work brought him success in the F3 and F2 arenas in the late 1960s. His first foray into Formula 1, with his friend Piers Courage driving, received a major set-back when the brewery heir was killed in Williams' car during the 1970 Dutch Grand Prix.

It took until 1978 before Williams got a strong foothold in Formula 1 and his team won its first Grand Prix, the British, the following year with Clay Regazzoni at the wheel of the winning car. In 1980 Alan Jones won the World Championship for Williams and Keke Rosberg was similarly mounted when he took the title two years later.

Williams' cars have achieved an enviable reputation for meticulous preparation and high standards of finish, qualities which mirror Frank's scrupulous approach to the F1 business. They are also well sponsored, mainly from Saudi Arabian sources, thanks to Williams' single-minded efforts on the commercial side of his business.

Frank Williams: meticulous.

43

Road to the top

Although it is possible to make the grade and gradually establish a reputation good enough to earn a position in a top Grand Prix team, the road to the top is strewn with pitfalls, both from the point of view of talent and finance. In an unavoidably expensive sport such as professional motor racing — relying as it does on costly equipment — having the necessary sponsorship available is a crucially important aspect of a driver's climb to prominence. He will certainly need it to make his mark at the lower levels of the sport, and its absence may even adversely affect his progress once he has made his name as an established driver.

Over the past decade several worthy Grand Prix drivers have failed to get a reasonable crack of the whip in F1, solely because they have not been able to raise the financial backing necessary. There are several top-line drivers who owe their positions in the limelight, at least in part, to generous sponsorship at an important moment. Money and talent are inseparable partners in the motor racing game.

There are many club racing categories in which it is possible for an aspiring star to cut his teeth, and many Grand Prix drivers first set out on the road to the top at the wheel of a modest saloon or sports car, such as a Ford Anglia or a Lotus Seven. However, over the last decade or so, with motor racing becoming steadily more popular and competitive, a clear-cut path has emerged along which it is virtually essential to tread in an attempt to become a Grand Prix driver.

Racing drivers' schools have helped, but their quality varies considerably. However, they allow the young enthusiast either to get the whole motor racing bug out of his system, or they help him to decide in favour of embarking on his own programme — in both cases, at relatively low cost.

The lowest rung on the ladder to the top is Formula Ford, a category devised in 1968 to cater for straightforward, single-seater racing cars with mildly tuned Cortina engines and road tyres. When the category first started there was a maximum price limit of £1,000 imposed by the regulations on completed cars. Now, most professional teams reckon that this modest category will require a £50,000 outlay for a season in the most important British championships. There are more than twenty national British FF championships at present, providing a varied menu of racing on different circuits. They all provide the up-and-coming stars with the opportunity to learn about car control, cut-and-thrust manoeuvring and race-craft in a hectic environment.

Those who have made the grade in Formula Ford will advance, providing they have got the finance, to Formula Ford 2000 (FF2000), a more exalted category using two litre Ford engines but also employing such refinements as racing 'slick' tyres and adjustable aerofoils — technical niceties they will encounter with increasing frequency as they move up the ladder. If they can snare a decent-sized commercial sponsor, a season in Formula 3 will be a possibility: this is an international category in which they will be driving, in effect, miniature Grand Prix cars with two litre engines developing around 165 bhp.

An additional attraction is that competitors will begin to come under the scrutiny of Grand Prix team managers as some of the major F3 events are held as supporting races to the Grands Prix. One only has to look through the list of winners of the Monaco F3 classic to appreciate how crucial success in these events can be to further progress: in 1972, for

Elio de Angelis

example, Patrick Depailler splashed to victory in an F3 Alpine-Renault. Six years later he was back, winning the Grand Prix itself in a car from the British Tyrrell stable. In 1964, Jackie Stewart ran away with that same F3 race, to equally good effect, and other bright-eyed youngsters who became top stars after winning the Monaco classic include Ronnie Peterson, Elio de Angelis and Didier Pironi.

Beyond Formula 3, the 'thinning out' process gets under way. While a handful of stars can successfully make the jump straight from F3 into the exalted heights of Grand Prix stardom, this often depends as much on finance as sheer talent. Ideally, of course, you need both! Stewart jumped the gap in 1965 successfully, but he was outstanding; so did Peterson and de Angelis (the latter aided by family wealth).

Formula 2 is the next category on the trail to Formula 1. These two litre, racing engined single-seaters develop in the order of 330 bhp-plus, quite sufficient to tell whether a driver has the stuff within him of which champions are made. Another advantage of F2 is that it attunes a driver to running longer races; often some F3 whizz-kids who jump straight into Grand Prix cars find themselves physically at sea. There is a world of distance between a 20-lap, 30-mile thrash round Brands Hatch in an F3 Ralt and 200 miles of hard racing at the wheel of a much heavier Grand Prix Lotus, Tyrrell or McLaren.

The European Formula 2 Championship attracts a degree of prestige and attention. It also produces a float of drivers who should be capable of handling a Grand Prix car with a couple of years' experience under their belts. Then it is the big jump, to 600 bhp, high technology single-seaters capable of 180 mph, but weighing no more than 540 kg. The drivers will

have to learn their F1 craft in frantic qualifying sessions, jostled by famous world champions, as they seek to perfect the technique required by the super-soft, one-lap 'qualifying tyres', the effect of which is to enable their cars to complete a fast lap during practice to gain an excellent starting-grid position.

Formula 1 is an extremely uncompromising world in which a chance fumbled is almost always a chance lost forever. Second chances do not come often, although it has to be said that one 1983 championship contender, Patrick Tambay, took three cracks at F1, each split by more than six months, before he made the grade. The Frenchman's experience, however, is very much the exception rather than the rule.

For the driver who has just missed making his mark in Formula 1, there's still potential for a professional career outside single-seaters. World championship sports car racing attracts an appreciable number of highly experienced and talented contenders who have either served out their useful career in F1, retired from it through choice or never quite made the grade.

However, it would be a great mistake to underestimate the qualities required for driving a Group C Porsche 956 turbo in a round of the World Endurance Championship. Apart from the fact that these sports car classic races can last for anything from six to twenty-four hours, the fastest cars are capable of speeds around the 200mph mark and they are frequently mixed with smaller capacity machines with far lower levels of performance.

Thus the potential hazards which stem from such speed differentials impose an additional strain on the drivers.

Didier Pironi

Events and competitions

The Formula 1 World Championship is generally acknowledged as the absolute pinnacle of international motor racing. It usually comprises between fourteen and sixteen races, the calendar starting in South America in February or March and finishing in Europe or North America towards the end of September or the beginning of October. The prize fund for such races is rigidly laid out in a commercial contract between the individual organisers and the Formula One Constructors' Association, on behalf of the competing teams.

A degree of masonic secrecy has shrouded the precise financial arrangements involved, but an individual race prize fund was $850,000 in 1983. Races a long way from Europe will have to contribute transportation costs for cars and equipment as well, a factor which has made the cost of staging events such as Long Beach, Argentina and South Africa approach the $1.5m mark.

The $850,000 prize fund is then split up in accordance with a complicated, yet reasonably equitable formula, which awards twenty per cent on the basis of the order in official qualifying for the race, forty-five per cent for the race result and the remaining thirty-five per cent in relation to aggregate performance over the two previous half years. Critics of the system say that the FOCA prize structure tends to favour the status quo and makes it very difficult for a newcomer to establish itself in the F1 business. That view, needless to say, is strenuously rejected by those current participants!

It is customary for a driver to receive between twenty and forty-five per cent of his car's earnings, the balance going to the team owner and a small percentage, between five and ten per cent, being channelled into an end-of-season bonus fund for the mechanics. Top drivers will have large

Rosberg in action and Lauda in the pits.

retainers, possibly paid by an independent personal sponsor such as Marlboro cigarettes or Parmalat, the Italian dairy food producer. Famous drivers like Niki Lauda, Keke Rosberg or Alain Prost will be able to earn up to $2m during a good year.

With a Grand Prix driver's earning life limited to six or seven good years, they would argue they need every penny they can get their hands on. At the opposite end of the scale, some of the junior drivers receive no retainers, pay their own expenses and wind up with a few thousand pounds at the end of the season — a reflection on the unreliabilty of their machines and consequent inability to earn much from the GP prize funds!

Outside Formula 1, the financial story is dramatically different. The European Formula 2 championship has just as much reliance on commercial sponsorship to make a season's programme financially viable for teams such as the British-based Ralt or March organisations. But here, more so than in Formula 1, the prize funds contribute a much smaller overall percentage of the category's earnings, a factor which makes outside sponsorship doubly important.

That trend is exaggerated further down the scale, notably in the British Formula 3 championship where £100,000 budgets are being expended on one car to chase individual prizes of only £1,000. The reality of that financial situation is that prize money will barely pay the tyre bill, let alone the other expenses of running the cars. Thus, in Formula 3, unless you are a wealthy amateur, outside sponsorship is a total necessity.

In North America, the CART series approaches its prize structure in a slightly different manner from Formula 1: it is a prize money only approach, with no payment on the basis of how a driver/car combination

has performed in the past. In essence, the further and faster you go, the more money you earn!

In the 1981 Indianapolis 500, Bobby Unser netted more than $299,000 for taking his place on the winner's rostrum — but the first retirement in the thirty-three car field, Mike Mosley's Eagle, still took home over $1,000, with a pro-rata prize fund between these two extremes. Interestingly, the American CART racing contenders make a big thing out of publicising just how much money they have made during the course of a season.

In 1981 top earner Rick Mears made $323,000 from prize funds alone (although he would have supplemented that from other sponsorship sources), but nobody in Europe has a clue what the 1982 world champion, Keke Rosberg, earned from his prize fund. In that respect, Formula 1 stands alone

Formula 2 in '83: A March (top) and a Ralt (LAT Photographic)

among big money sports: golf, tennis and other major sports have properly published prize funds for each event. Grand Prix racing, for some unfathomable reason, does not.

Venues

One of the great things about international motor racing is the wide variety of circuits used throughout the world. They range from the flat, yet demanding, swooping curves of Silverstone — former wartime RAF base and regular scene of the British Grand Prix — to the ups and downs of Brands Hatch in Kent; from the twists ands turns through the streets of Monaco to the undulating high-speed corners of the Osterreichring, venue of the Austrian Grand prix.

The British Grand Prix alternates between Silverstone and Brands Hatch, but Britain also has another splendid facility at Donington — a fine circuit in a tree-lined park near Derby — and other converted airfields at Thruxton and Snetterton. The most recent purpose-built race-track to be constructed from scratch is the rather clinical Paul Ricard facility, situated in the sun-soaked scrubland of the Camargue, just above Bandol in the South of France. The cost of this

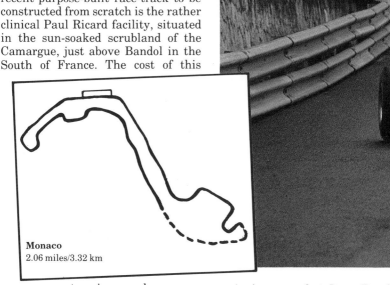

Monaco
2.06 miles/3.32 km

enormous enterprise was borne personally by pastis millionaire Paul Ricard, but for the last decade there has been a tendency to emulate Monaco and stage new races round the streets of important cities.

For true romantics, Monaco will always be the jewel in Grand Prix racing's crown, but Long Beach and Detroit both proved that they could organise street races which provided more interesting and demanding circuits than the Mediterranean Principality. The great advantage of such races, of course, is that the organisers do not have expensive circuits to

52

1983 Monaco Grand Prix (LAT Photographic)

maintain in between races. A few hours after the chequered flag has fluttered, armies of construction workers swing into action reconverting the city streets from race-tracks to boulevards.

Long Beach, which has recently taken the decision to switch from

Buenos Aires
3.71 miles/5.97 km

Venues/2

Formula 1 to CART for 1984 on the grounds of expense, honed this process of transformation to a fine art over the past seven years. The Long Beach Grand Prix was over by five o'clock on a Sunday evening and by Monday morning there was precious little evidence to suggest that this Californian coastal city was much more than a quiet, retirement suburb of Los Angeles.

Changing views on circuit safety and security have been responsible for historic, classical circuits undergoing major transformations over the past decade, in order that they may con-

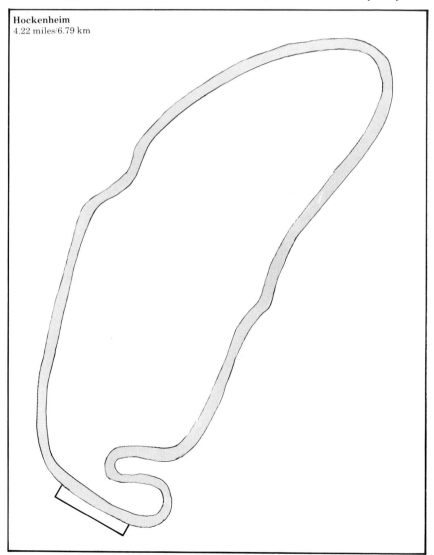

Hockenheim
4.22 miles/6.79 km

tinue to host international events. The 14 mile Nürburgring, home of the German Grand Prix since the 1930s, has now been superseded by a brand new track, adjacent to the old circuit, but blending its old character with all the up-to-date facilities one could ever require.

The Spa-Francorchamps circuit, home of the Belgian Grand Prix until 1970, has just been reopened following extensive revision. It hosted the Belgian Grand Prix again in 1983, and earned unanimous acclaim from everybody involved in the F1 business.

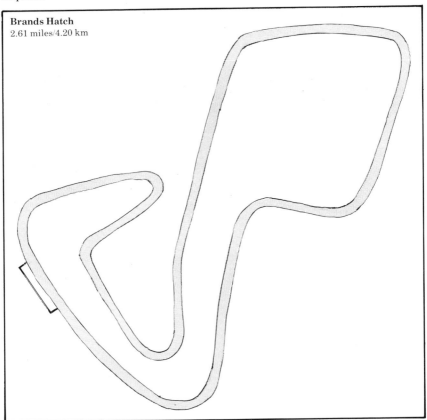

Brands Hatch
2.61 miles/4.20 km

Technology

In the space of twenty years, the Grand Prix car has developed from a rather crude, if effective, device by engineering standards, to a highly sophisticated machine built almost to aerospace specifications of quality and detail. In the chassis, for instance, modern cars combine strength with lightness to such an extent that drivers now emerge unscathed from accidents which, in the recent past, would have caused them serious injuries.

At the start of the 1960s most Formula 1 cars were straightforward tubular steel spaceframes, on to which either hand-crafted steel or glass-fibre bodywork was attached. Driver safety was limited to the provision of rollover bars, most of which simply paid lip service to the regulations: most failed to reach above the driver's head (rendering them useless in a major accident), were not braced (so they would collapse anyway), and the fact that seat harnesses were regarded in some quarters as 'cissy' meant that dreadful injuries could be sustained by a driver 'half falling out' of a wayward machine.

The notion that it was better to be flung clear than stay with the car was foremost in many people's minds. The concept of safety was treated with a degree of incomprehension, even thinly veiled scorn. Motor racing was a dangerous business and that was an end to it.

In the 1980s, as much attention goes into the business of driver protection when it comes to designing a Grand Prix chassis as the car's ability to fulfil its performance requirements. The basic regulations round which an F1 car must be built are now so stringent that it is almost surprising that one looks even slightly different from another. The fact of the matter is that, in most cases, today's F1 cars are enormously safe pieces of equipment.

Some would argue, of course, that they have to be bearing in mind the endless upward spiral of lap speeds over the past two decades.

Today's F1 car is built to regulations which demand a minimum weight of 540kg. The central monocoque, or fuselage, sections are often built out of lightweight aluminium alloy sheet, but, increasingly, sophisticated materials such as carbon-fibre are employed as well. A number of cars today employ a Nomex honeycomb/carbon-fibre composite construction which enables high levels of strength to be sustained while keeping the overall structure as light as possible.

Team Lotus were among the first to employ this form of construction and have built more than a dozen chassis over the past three years using this system. Despite some daunting accidents on the tracks, they have yet to write one off completely. The use of carbon-fibre provides the stiffness of an alloy sheet monocoque with a one-third weight saving — or one and a half times the strength for the same weight. In the split-second world of Grand Prix racing, where weight means fractions of seconds per lap, such technology has been a godsend for most top designers.

The highest point on a Grand Prix car is the rollover bar, a far cry from the spindly 'fuse wire' concoctions of the 1960s. Nowadays it is a substantial, firm, fully braced hoop of steel, capable of supporting the full weight of the car without distorting.

Specially strengthened footwells are required as a matter of course, to minimise the possibility of frontal deformation, and there has to be a special nose section ahead of the footwell which is designed to crumple gradually in the event of an accident. This further minimises the potential damage to the front of the car.

Fire has always been a major hazard

1970 Lotus driven by Jochen Rindt (LAT Photographic)

Technology/2

in motor racing, particularly in the days when steel fuel tanks were hung onto the outside of the old spaceframe chassis; it was simply regarded as one of the necessary risks of the sport. But a spate of much-publicised, fiery accidents in the early 1970s gave rise to new regulations which required that fuel tanks be covered with protective, deformable structures. But up until 1978 cars were still being built with more than one tank: there were usually two, one either side of the driver, feeding into a collector tank before being directed into the engine's fuel injection system.

Now that has all been changed. Single, central fuel cells are obligatory and take the form of foam-filled, aircraft-style rubber cells fitted into virtually 'bullet proof' containers in the middle of the car. There is very little possibility of fuel spillage with this sort of layout and, with a minimum of pipes and fuel lines between the main supply source and the engine, not much chance of minor leaks arising.

Hand-in-hand with the high standard of chassis development, F1 engine technology has raced ahead. The current three litre Formula 1 started in 1966, the rules allowing a provision to use supercharged versions of obsolete F1 engines from the supplanted one and a half litre formula.

Nobody followed this line of technical development for over eleven years, until Renault arrived on the scene with its ambitious turbocharged one and a half litre V6, a powerful little engine which used the principle of harnessing the exhaust gases to increase the pressure at which the fuel/air mixture was forced into the engine. Although this system was not 'supercharging' to the letter of the regulation, it was tacitly accepted as a method of 'forced induction' and only

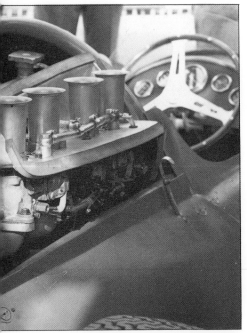

when the French power unit started to produce worthwhile results did the opposition begin to object that the engine was strictly illegal.

By then, however, such objections were lost in the helter-skelter of enthusiasm to get onto the turbocharged bandwagon. As a result, 1984 will see engines from Porsche and Honda supplementing those already produced by BMW, Renault, Ferrari, Alfa Romeo and the small British Hart organisation. The era of the small, specialist Formula 1 team may well be over and Grand Prix racing looks set to become the preserve of the major manufacturer once again, just as it was in the mid-1950s.

At the end of the day, motor racing may survive as a branch of show business, but it also has a major role to fulfil as a technical laboratory for future ideas which may find their way onto the public road.

Engines: 1960 Ensign (top) and a 1983 Renault (LAT Photographic)

Lotus

People in the media

Murray Walker

To those who follow Grand Prix racing from the comfort of their armchairs at home, the face (and voice) of Formula 1 is Murray Walker, the BBC's ebullient, long-time commentator whose frantically enthusiastic tones recount the action from all corners of the world. A man with a passionate and overwhelming interest in cars, motorcycles and motor racing in any form, Murray has recently retired from his senior position with a West End advertising agency to concentrate full-time on commentating, his hobby for many years but now, in effect, his full-time, all abiding occupation.

Murray Walker's enthusiasm for the sport dates back to his childhood. His father, Graham, was one of Britain's most accomplished international motorcycle racers between the wars and, as a small child, Murray was taken round with his parents to many international events during the 1930s. Eventually he became involved in commentating on motorcycle events, through his father, in the late

1940s. Murray also tried his hand at motorcycle racing but, by his own admission, it was 'only a bit of dabbling at club level'.

Throughout the 1950s, Murray concentrated his commentating on the two-wheeled branch of the sport, gradually moving into the car racing side during the 1960s and taking over as the BBC's man when Raymond Baxter finally moved on to other things in the early 1970s. Murray Walker's infectious enthusiasm spills over obviously into his commentaries: he never seems bored, always finds something interesting to talk about — and perhaps, according to his critics, keeps talking for too much of the television transmission.

'I've been told by my colleagues at the BBC that I should keep quiet a little more, perhaps allowing the viewers to just watch the cars and listen to the engines . . . I think this is probably a justifiable criticism, but it's not always as easy as it may appear to those on the outside!'

James Hunt

Extrovert, outspoken and fun-loving,

James Hunt

James Hunt won the World Championship for McLaren in 1976 in a cliff-hanging finale over the reigning title holder, Niki Lauda. After a spectacular early career in Formula Ford and Formula 3, where he spent as much time crashing as winning due to his sheer enthusiasm to get the best out of less-than-competitive machinery, Hunt matured into an accomplished Grand Prix ace of considerable stature.

After his championship success, Hunt never quite scaled the same pinnacles of achievement, partly because the McLaren team failed to adapt quickly enough to 'ground effect' technology in 1977, and James began to lose his heart for the F1 business. By the start of 1979 it seemed likely that he would race only for another season, but he quit abruptly mid-way through the year, disillusioned because (so it seemed to him) the nature of the new breed of 'ground effect' car was diluting the driver's contribution to the overall competitive package.

Since that time, he has been Murray

Jackie Stewart

Walker's partner in the BBC TV commentary team. Relaxed, critical and opinionated, James's great strength is that he knows most of the drivers personally, can relate to their problems and can explain the technical aspects of their performance with a degree of straightforward clarity. He tends to be a little partisan in some of his observations, but many people feel that adds a little extra spice to the whole presentation. Away from motor racing, Hunt lives near London and spends a lot of his time playing squash and golf to high standards.

Jackie Stewart
Apart from his prowess behind the wheel of a Grand Prix car, Jackie Stewart has developed into an articulate, sensitive commentator, carrying out a considerable amount of television work in North America over the past few years. As much at home talking at senior level in a company boardroom as behind a microphone, Stewart's professional versatility has helped educate the American viewing public to the niceties of European Grand Prix racing.

Statistics

World Championship

1950
1 N Farina
2 J-M Fangio
3 L Fagioli
4 L Rosier
5 A Ascari
6 Prince Bira

1951
1 J-M Fangio
2 A Ascari
3 F Gonzales
4 N Farina
5 L Villoresi
6 P Taruffi

1952
1 A Ascari
2 N Farina
3 P Taruffi
4 =R Fischer
   M Hawthorn
6 R Manzon

1953
1 A Ascari
2 J-M Fangio
3 N Farina
4 M Hawthorn
5 L Villoresi
6 F Gonzales

1954
1 J-M Fangio
2 F Gonzales
3 M Hawthorn
4 M Trintignant
5 K Kling
6 H Herrmann

1955
1 J-M Fangio
2 S Moss
3 E Castelotti
4 M Trintignant
5 N Farina
6 P Taruffi

1956
1 J-M Fangio
2 S Moss
3 P Collins
4 J Behra
5 E Castelotti
6 =P Frere
   F Godia

1957
1 J-M Fangio
2 S Moss
3 L Musso
4 M Hawthorn
5 T Brooks
6 H Schell

1958
1 M Hawthorn
2 S Moss
3 T Brooks
4 R Salvadori
5 =H Schell
   P Collins

1959
1 J Brabham
2 T Brooks
3 S Moss
4 P Hill
5 M Trintignant
6 B McLaren

1960
1 J Brabham
2 B McLaren
3 S Moss
4 I Ireland
5 P Hill
6 W von Trips

1961
1 P Hill
2 W von Trips
3 =S Moss
   D Gurney
5 R Ginther
6 I Ireland

1962
1 G Hill
2 J Clark
3 B McLaren
4 J Surtees
5 D Gurney
6 P Hill

1963
1 J Clark
2 G Hill
3 R Ginther
4 J Surtees
5 D Gurney
6 B McLaren

1964
1 J Surtees
2 G Hill
3 J Clark
4 =L Bandini
   R Ginther
6 D Gurney

1965
1 J Clark
2 G Hill
3 J Stewart
4 D Gurney
5 J Surtees
6 L Bandini

1966
1 J Brabham
2 J Surtees
3 J Rindt
4 D Hulme
5 G Hill
6 J Clark

1967
1 D Hulme
2 J Brabham
3 J Clark
4 J Surtees
5 C Amon
6 P Rodriguez

1968
1 G Hill
2 J Stewart
3 D Hulme
4 J Ickx
5 B McLaren
6 P Rodriguez

1969
1 J Stewart
2 J Ickx
3 B McLaren
4 J Rindt
5 J-P Beltoise
6 D Hulme

1970
1 J Rindt
2 J Ickx
3 C Regazzoni
4 D Hulme
5 =J Brabham
   J Stewart

1971
1 J Stewart
2 R Peterson
3 F Cevert
4 =J Ickx
   J Siffert
6 E Fittipaldi

1972
1 E Fittipaldi
2 J Stewart
3 D Hulme
4 J Ickx
5 P Revson
6 F Cevert

1973
1 J Stewart
2 E Fittipaldi
3 R Peterson
4 F Cevert
5 P Revson
6 D Hulme

1974
1 E Fittipaldi
2 C Regazzoni
3 J Sheckter
4 N Lauda
5 R Peterson
6 C Reutemann

1975
1 N Lauda
2 E Fittipaldi
3 C Reutemann
4 J Hunt
5 C Regazzoni
6 C Pace

1976
1 J Hunt
2 N Lauda
3 J Scheckter
4 P Depailler
5 C Regazzoni
6 M Andretti

1977
1 N Lauda
2 J Sheckter
3 M Andretti
4 C Reutemann
5 J Hunt
6 J Mass

1978
1 M Andretti
2 R Peterson
3 C Reutemann
4 N Lauda
5 P Depailler
6 J Watson

1979
1 J Sheckter
2 G Villeneuve
3 A Jones
4 J Laffite
5 C Regazzoni
6 P Depailler

1980
1 A Jones
2 N Piquet
3 C Reutemann
4 J Laffite
5 D Pironi
6 R Arnoux

1981
1 N Piquet
2 C Reutemann
3 A Jones
4 J Laffite
5 A Prost
6 J Watson

1982
1 K Rosberg
2 =J Watson
    D Pironi
4 A Prost
5 N Lauda
6 R Arnoux

1983
1 N Piquet
2 A Prost
3 R Arnoux
4 P Tambay
5 K Rosberg
6 J Watson

European Formula 2 Championship
Winners (since inception in 1967)

1967	**1976**
J Ickx	J-P Jabouille
1968	**1977**
J-P Beltoise	R Arnoux
1969	**1978**
J Servoz-Gavin	B Giacomelli
1970	**1979**
C Regazzoni	M Surer
1971	**1980**
R Peterson	B Henton
1972	**1981**
M Hailwood	G Lees
1973	**1982**
J-P Jarier	C Fabi
1974	**1983**
P Depailler	J Palmer
1975	
J Laffite	

Car Constructors championship
Inaugurated 1958

1958	**1971**
Vanwall	Tyrrell-Ford Cosworth
1959	**1972**
Cooper-Coventry Climax	Lotus-Ford Cosworth
1960	**1973**
Cooper-Coventry Climax	Lotus-Ford Cosworth
1961	**1974**
Ferrari	McLaren-Ford Cosworth
1962	**1975**
BRM	Ferrari
1963	**1976**
Lotus-Coventry Climax	Ferrari
1964	**1977**
Ferrari	Ferrari
1965	**1978**
Lotus-Coventry Climax	Lotus-Ford Cosworth
1966	**1979**
Brabham-Repco	Ferrari
1967	**1980**
Brabham-Repco	Williams-Ford Cosworth
1968	**1981**
Lotus-Ford Cosworth	Williams-Ford Cosworth
1969	**1982**
Matra-Ford Cosworth	Ferrari
1970	**1983**
Lotus-Ford Cosworth	Ferrari

Brands Hatch